"Not a sour note. Not a lost chord. Not a misplaced phrase."
—*The Toronto Star*

"*2 Pianos 4 Hands* is destined to travel far, not only across Canada, but also within international cultural circles."
—*Variety*

"Be glad Ted Dykstra and Richard Greenblatt suffered tormented child-hoods. Be thankful, in fact. Because if they hadn't, odds are *2 Pianos 4 Hands*, their hilarious show, might never have happened."
—*The Washington Post*

"A shining *2 Pianos 4 Hands* is about the rigors of mastering the instrument, but it's for anyone with a dream."
—*The Los Angeles Times*

"A damn fine way to treat two Steinways."
—*The Independent* (UK)

"Enormously enjoyable."
—*The Times of London*

"*2 Pianos 4 Hands* is a night to savour."
—*The Sydney Morning Herald*

**** "Magical! Superb! Laugh-out-loud funny! Poignant! Perfection! This is the last time that *2 Pianos 4 Hands* is coming our way before Ted Dykstra and Richard Greenblatt retire the show. Don't miss these fare-well performances."
—Paula Citron, *The Globe and Mail* (2011)

"A concerto of musical mayhem."
—Alex Reynolds, *CHCH News*

2 PIANOS 4 HANDS

2P4H
2 PIANOS 4 HANDS

BY TED DYKSTRA & RICHARD GREENBLATT

PLAYWRIGHTS CANADA PRESS
TORONTO

Playwrights Canada Press
202-269 Richmond St. W.
Toronto, ON M5V 1X1
416.703.0013 • info@playwrightscanada.com • www.playwrightscanada.com

For professional or amateur production rights, please contact:
Marquis Entertainment
312-73 Richmond Street W., Toronto, ON M5H 4E8, Canada
416.960.9123
info@marquisent.ca, www.marquisent.ca, www.2pianos4hands.com

We acknowledge the financial support of the Canada Council for the Arts, the Ontario Arts Council, the Ontario Media Development Corporation, and the Government of Canada through the Canada Book Fund for our publishing activities.

 Canada Council **Conseil des Arts** 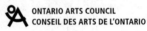 **ONTARIO ARTS COUNCIL**
for the Arts **du Canada** **CONSEIL DES ARTS DE L'ONTARIO**

Cover and book design by Blake Sproule

LIBRARY AND ARCHIVES CANADA CATALOGUING IN PUBLICATION
Dykstra, Ted
    2 pianos 4 hands / Ted Dykstra and Richard Greenblatt.

A play.
Issued also in electronic formats.
ISBN 978-1-77091-092-8

    I. Greenblatt, Richard, 1952- II. Title. III. Title: Two pianos
four hands.

PS8607.Y59T86 2012   C812'.6   C2012-904501-2

First edition: November 2012
Printed and bound in Canada by Marquis Book Printing, Montreal

Many people have asked us why it's taken over fifteen years and over five thousand performances in some two hundred cities on five continents to publish this script after its original opening at the Tarragon Theatre in Toronto in the spring of 1996.

Maybe because this is a piece that is inimitably meant to be performed rather than read. Maybe because it was created as a collective of two, stemming from anecdotes, memories, dreams, and nightmares, and only written down later as a chronicle of what we improvised. Maybe because the music played in the show is so inextricably linked to its theatrical essence and which cannot, almost by definition, be communicated with words. For whatever reason, we are very happy to present this now as a record of the work.

Whenever we perform it, we cannot help but make small changes. It is as if certain jokes or lines of dialogue have an expiration date, after which they go "off." This version is simply the latest incarnation, after our runs in Toronto and Ottawa in 2011–2012. We have no doubt that if and/or when we perform it again, there will be similar small changes.

We are indebted to many people who helped in the development of this piece. But we dedicate this play to our piano teachers—Dr. Lilian Upright of Edmonton and the late Professor Dorothy Morton of Montreal—who were our other mothers.

And to all piano teachers everywhere.

—Richard Greenblatt & Ted Dykstra

Ted and his piano teacher, Dr. Lilian Upright.
Photo by Beatrice Campbell.

Richard at the first day of rehearsals, 1996.
Photo by Beatrice Campbell.

Ted and Richard in front of the Great Canadian Theatre
Company, Ottawa, during their first Canadian tour, 1996.
Photo by Beatrice Campbell.

FOREWORD
BY THE RIGHT HONOURABLE ADRIENNE CLARKSON

I loved *2 Pianos 4 Hands* from the first time I saw it in 1996 at the Tarragon Theatre in Toronto. My feelings about the piano, about music, about satisfying my demanding parents, seemed to be refracted in the kaleidoscopic vision of Ted Dykstra and Richard Greenblatt.

I felt that they had been luckier than me: my teacher was not like theirs. Unfortunately, I was subjected to an antique vestal virgin called Miss Jamieson on Stewart Street in downtown Ottawa. Walking to the lessons after leaving class at Elgin Street Public School, I used to put one foot in front of the other, toe to heel, in order to get there as slowly as possible—so as not to hear her thumping time while the student before me was playing, and to put off as long as possible having to peer into her densely powdered, highly rouged, and wrinkled face with its three hairy moles. This vision was topped by wispy white hair, tied up in a bun inexplicably covered with a black hairnet. She seemed to have a perpetual running sore on her neck, which she attacked with a flowered handkerchief of some indefinable material. I was always somewhat worried that I would catch something from it but I kept knowledge of this from my mother, who was paranoid about germs. I had only to say that someone had sneezed near me at school for her to want to keep me at home the next day. For some perverse reason, I never mentioned the handkerchief and the running sore as an excuse to get out of my piano lessons.

I can see the old upright piano jammed against the wall and the small bay window to the right. Miss Jamieson inhabited the top half of a duplex and out of the corner of my eye, through the seasons, I could see snow-covered branches, burgeoning green leaves, and then the magic red and yellow of the maples turning colour. None of this was any solace for the forty-five minutes I spent in Miss Jamieson's presence each week. To make matters worse, she thought that my brother was a hidden musical genius. Every second sentence began with, "Your brother..." I knew that my brother had better technique, more willpower to practise, and was probably going to be a prodigy. And at the age of eight, I knew that playing the piano was not going to be my way to any earthly spotlight. Nor did my parents delude themselves into thinking this. They simply gave me the dollar a week for my lesson because they thought that, like ballet, it would somehow render me more graceful, socially adept, and correct my posture slump.

My mother loved the piano and played by heart. She did everything with great verve and instinct with absolutely no training. She could play Chopin's Nocturne in B Flat from memory, and if that had been the only thing she had to play, she could have filled concert halls with it. She also could knit anything just by looking at a picture and making up the pattern in her head. She was a kind of idiot savant, which I only learned to appreciate many, many years later. On days when I would come home from school and hear her playing Chopin, I knew it was going to be a better day than most. From her I learned the very basic thing about music: that it can be great solace in time of trouble.

When I saw Ted and Richard perform for the first time, all of these memories came rushing back, and when I think of their performance (I later went to two more in two different venues) I realized that playing the piano was not just about music, not just about playing "The Happy Farmer," not just about your parents, but about what life wiggles in front of you as a promise and what it may or may not deliver.

HISTORY

In 1994 Ted and Richard formed Talking Fingers to write and work-shop their new script, *2 Pianos 4 Hands*. The play was subsequently programmed as part of Tarragon Theatre's 1995–'96 season in Toronto and premiered in April 1996 to rave reviews and sold-out houses. Talking Fingers and the Tarragon shared the 1996 Dora Mavor Moore Award for Outstanding Production, and Ted and Richard received the prestigious Floyd S. Chalmers Canadian Play Award—Canada's national playwriting award—that same year.

Immediately following the close of the premiere run in Toronto, Ted and Richard embarked on a national tour. They travelled from coast to coast with the show, stopping back at the Tarragon for a second run in the fall of 1996, and concluding in Vancouver in September of 1997 at the Vancouver Playhouse.

In October of 1997, backed by a team of producers including David and Ed Mirvish, *2 Pianos 4 Hands* opened off-Broadway at the Promenade Theater. The production was widely acclaimed and ran for six months before transferring to the Kennedy Center in Washington, DC, in the spring of 1998. Ted and Richard returned to Toronto later that sum-mer and again played to sold-out houses, this time at the historic Royal Alexandra Theatre, with Mirvish Productions.

The show had its European premiere at the Birmingham Repertory Theatre in the spring of 1999, a production that transferred later that fall to the Comedy Theatre in the West End of London.

Since then, Ted and Richard have twice reunited to perform in Toronto with Marquis Entertainment/Talking Fingers/Mirvish Productions, twice toured to Japan, where they have performed in Tokyo and toured throughout the country, and in 2011–'12 embarked on a farewell tour that included visits to Ottawa and Vancouver.

There have been many other productions with other actors, both male and female, in Canada and across the globe.

Since its premiere, *2 Pianos 4 Hands* has had more than four thousand performances at two hundred different theatres throughout Canada, the US, the UK, Japan, Australia, Hong Kong, New Zealand, South Africa, and beyond. Nearly two million people have seen the play on five continents worldwide, making it one of the most successful Canadian plays ever.

For more information about *2 Pianos 4 Hands*, please visit the official show website: www.2pianos4hands.com and www.marquisent.ca.

Ted and Richard at their first costume fitting, Tarragon Theatre, Toronto, 1996.
Photo by Beatrice Campbell.

2 Pianos 4 Hands was originally produced in April 1996 by the Tarragon Theatre, Toronto, in association with Talking Fingers Inc., with the following cast:

Ted: Ted Dykstra
Richard: Richard Greenblatt

The production was directed by Ted Dykstra and Richard Greenblatt with Andy McKim as consulting director, production design by Steve Lucas, and stage management by Beatrice Campbell.

The play was first produced off-Broadway in October 1997 by Mirvish Productions with Ben Sprecher and William P. Miller, and featured the following cast:

Ted: Ted Dykstra
Richard: Richard Greenblatt

The production was directed by Gloria Muzio with Andy McKim as Associate Director, set and costume design by Steve Lucas, lighting design by Tharon Musser, and stage management by Beatrice Campbell.

2 Pianos 4 Hands is represented by Robert Richardson and Colin Rivers at Marquis Entertainment Inc., www.marquisent.ca.

CLASSICAL MUSIC FEATURED
IN 2 PIANOS 4 HANDS

ACT I

Concerto in D minor, 1st Movement (J.S. Bach)
Sonatina No. 6 in F Major (Beethoven)
Sonata Facile in C Major, 1st Movement (Mozart)
Sonata for One Piano, Four Hands in D Major, 1st Movement (Mozart)
In der Halle des Bergkonigs, Peer Gynt Suite 1 (Edward Grieg)
Concerto in D minor, 1st Movement (J.S. Bach)

ACT II

Prelude in D flat Major (Chopin)
Leyenda (I. Albeniz)
Rondo for Two Pianos, Four Hands in C Major (Chopin)
Fantasiestucke No. 2 (Schumann)
Pathetique Sonata No. 8 in C minor, 1st and 2nd Movements
(Beethoven)
Ballade No. 2 in F Major (Chopin)
Mephisto Waltz No. 1 (Franz Listz)
A Medley of Pop Tunes
Impromptu in A flat (Schubert)
Concerto in D minor, 1st Movement (J.S. Bach)

ACT I

IN THE BEGINNING

RICHARD and TED enter dressed in concert tails, come to a spot at centre stage, and bow to the audience. RICHARD turns to bow to TED but TED has already left the centre to go to his piano. An awkward moment. RICHARD goes to his piano. They sit.

Something is wrong. TED is not happy. He makes his way to RICHARD's piano and whispers something. After a short conference, RICHARD gets up and offers his piano to TED. They sit again.

TED goes once again to RICHARD. After another more spirited discussion, RICHARD goes to the other piano. They pick up their benches and exchange them. Apologizing to the audience, they sit again.

They are ready to begin. TED adjusts his bench several times, shifting each time just as RICHARD is about to play. Finally, TED rolls his head to loosen it up. RICHARD's head sinks down to the keyboard. TED plays a low note to get RICHARD's attention. RICHARD looks up and TED motions to him that he's ready to go. Finally, they begin to play the first movement of Bach's D Minor Piano Concerto.

Everything is going swimmingly until about a minute in. One of them starts a different section. They are not together. They look at each other in horror. The piece is disintegrating. It grinds to a halt and TED plays two finishing chords. They look at the audience, at each other, and at their hands.

Out of this abyss, TED raises one finger. It descends on middle C and he plays a C major scale.

TED   C Major: ONE FINGER, ONE HAND, ONE OCTAVE.

RICHARD   D Flat Major: WITH FINGERING, ONE OCTAVE, ONE HAND.

TED   D Major: WITH FINGERING, ONE OCTAVE, TWO HANDS.

RICHARD   E Flat Major: TWO OCTAVES, TWO HANDS, SLIGHTLY FASTER.

TED   E Major: FOUR OCTAVES, QUITE FAST.

RICHARD   F Major: CONTRARY MOTION PATTERN, EVEN FASTER.

TED   F Sharp Minor: HARMONIC, FOUR OCTAVES.

RICHARD   G Major: ARPEGGIO, FOUR OCTAVES.

TED   A Flat Major: BROKEN CHORDS, TWO OCTAVES.

RICHARD   A Minor: MELODIC MINOR, FOUR OCTAVES.

TED   B Flat Diminished Seventh: BROKEN CHORDS, TWO OCTAVES.

RICHARD   B Major: SYNCOPATED OCTAVES.

They are now cooking with gas. In a last, glorious explosion they join forces, pounding out a heart-stopping succession of octaves in a grand finale kind of way.

After the last crashing octave, the well-known and terribly simple bass pattern to "Heart and Soul," that even people who have never had a lesson seem to know how to play, is heard. The players take us through different styles and keys of this old chestnut, taking it to places few have dared to go. They move into "Chopsticks" and the knuckle-roll song—more favourites. The arrangement finishes with them playing a simple scale with one finger, a third apart, for two octaves, ending with trills and leading into...

LESSONS I

RICHARD *plays "I Hear a Bird," ignoring the rests.*

TED   *(throughout)* Rests, Richie. No, rests. Richie, rests. Richie... you're too young to use the pedal.

RICHARD *takes his foot off the sustain pedal.*

TED *plays "In My Little Birch Canoe."*

RICHARD   Curve your fingers. *(TED does, raising his wrists.)* Lower your wrists. *(TED does, straightening his fingers.)* Curve your fingers. Lower your wrists. Curve your fingers. Lower your wrists. *(singing in time to the music)* Curve your fingers and lower your wrists at the same time, Teddy.

RICHARD *plays "By the Stream."*

SISTER LOYOLA

TED   *(in response to a misplayed note)* B flat, dear. B flat.

> RICHARD *tries to comprehend his error by playing the discordant notes over and over.*

Stop playing. Stop playing. Stop playing.

> TED *makes his way over to* RICHARD. *He is now Sister Loyola, who massages her left eye throughout the scene.*

How many flats are there in the key signature, Richard?

RICHARD   Four, Sister Loyola.

TED   Mmm. And they are?

RICHARD   Um… B, um… E, um… C—

TED   No. Just down a little spacey from C.

RICHARD   A!

TED   Yes. And…

RICHARD   D!! B-E-A-D! BEAD!

TED   BEAD. Yes, good.

RICHARD   BEAD!

TED   Yes.

RICHARD   BEAD!!

TED   Very good, dear. So, what key are we in, Richard? *(He draws a blank.)* How do we know what key we're in, dear? Remember?

RICHARD   Oh! You take the last flat—

TED   No, dear. The second-last flat.

RICHARD   Second-last flat—

TED   Yes, which is what?

RICHARD   A! A flat! We're in A flat!

TED   Almost, dear. Is this a happy-sounding song or a sad-sounding song? *(another blank)* Does it have a happy sound or does it have a sad sound?

RICHARD   *(RICHARD plays a short section.)* A sad sound.

TED   Yes. And when it's sad, it's…?

RICHARD   Minor!

TED   Yes. Very good, dear. Minor is sad. Minor is dark and gloomy. Whereas major is—

BOTH   —happy.

TED   So. If this were a happy-sounding song then we would be in…?

RICHARD   A.

TED   A what?

RICHARD   A flat.

TED   A flat what?

RICHARD   A flat minor!

TED   No, major, Richard!!

RICHARD   Major.

TED   Yes?

RICHARD   Yes.

TED   But it's not a happy-sounding song—

RICHARD   Nope.

TED   It's a sad-sounding song—

RICHARD   Yep.

TED   So we're not in a major key.

RICHARD   Nope.

TED   We're in a minor key.

RICHARD   Yep.

TED   And the relative minor of A flat major is…? *(another blank)* How do we find the relative minor of a major key, dear? *(blank)* We've done this. Remember? We go… (TED *points down.)*

RICHARD   Down!!

TED   How far? *(blank)* Oh, Richard. Three. Three semitones. Father, Son, and Holy Ghost.

RICHARD   *(going down from A flat)* Baruch atah Adonai.

TED   Whatever, dear.

RICHARD   F. F flat. We're in F flat minor!

TED   *(losing it)* Not F flat, dear! Just F! F minor! *(beat)* Okay.

RICHARD   Okay.

TED   Now, F minor has four flats.

RICHARD   Yes, Sister.

TED   And what are they, dear?

RICHARD   Um… B, um… E, um… C—

TED   No, Richard. What's the saying that we use that helps us remember what the order of the flats is?

RICHARD   Battle Ends And Down Goes Father Charles.

TED   Charles' Father.

RICHARD   Charles' Father.

TED   And the order of the sharps?

RICHARD   Charles' Father Goes Down—

TED   Charles' Father does not go down! Father Charles Goes Down—

RICHARD   —And Ends Battle.

TED   What's the word that spells the spaces in the treble clef?

RICHARD	"Face."
TED	The bass clef?
RICHARD	All Cows Eat Grass.
TED	Lines in the treble clef?
RICHARD	Every Good Boy Deserves Fudge.
TED	In the bass clef?
RICHARD	Good Boys Deserve Fudge Always. Sister Loyola?
TED	No, you can't have any fudge, dear. *(beat)* So. What key are we in, Richard? *(RICHARD draws a blank.)* Sister Loyola has a little pain in her left eye, dear. She's just going to go upstairs and have a little lie down and a cup of tea. You keep trying to figure out what key we're in and when your lesson's over you can let yourself out.

> *TED sits at his piano and begins to play "Our Band Goes To Town."*

BERKOFF I

RICHARD	Okay. Okay. Teddy. Stop playing. Stop playing. Stop playing.
TED	It sounded a lot better at home.
RICHARD	Okay, Teddy, why don't you try counting out loud while you play?
TED	Mr. Berkoff?

RICHARD   Count out loud while you play.

           TED plays, counting continuously. He's at twenty by the
           time RICHARD stops him.

           Whoa, whoa, whoa.

TED   That's hard.

RICHARD   Teddy. What's the time signature of the piece?

TED   Yes.

RICHARD   The time signature, Ted?

TED   Four... two fours... four over four... forty-four.

RICHARD   Didn't your last teacher go over this with you? *(TED shrugs.)*
           Didn't she teach you about time signatures?

TED   Well sort of, I guess.

RICHARD   Didn't she make sure that you understood the concept of
           time?

TED   Whoa.

RICHARD   Well what the heck did she do?

TED   She usually just went upstairs for a little lie down and a cup
           of tea, / and when my lesson was over I would let myself
           out and my dad would get mad at me.

RICHARD   *(overlaps with line above)* I don't believe this. Okay. Okay.
           Teddy, we call the time signature of this piece four-four.

TED   Four-four.

RICHARD   Now. It's also called common time. That's why you some-
           times see a C at the beginning of the piece.

TED   Oh boy.

RICHARD   But we'll just call it four-four for now.

TED   Four-four for now.

RICHARD   Just four-four.

TED   Just four-four.

RICHARD   Four-four.

TED   Four-four.

RICHARD   Okay.

TED   Okay.

RICHARD   Now. Four-four means…?

TED   Four.

RICHARD   Four what?

TED   For the music.

RICHARD   Teddy. The top four means…?

TED   The best ones.

RICHARD   Okay, okay. In a time signature, the top number tells us
           how many beats there are in each bar. The bottom number
           tells us what each one of those beats is worth. So, if we're in
           four-four that means there are how many what's in a what?

TED   What?

RICHARD   How many beats in the bar?

TED   *(by accident)* Four?

RICHARD   Yes! Four! Very good! Now the bottom four tells us what
             each one of those four beats is worth… and that is?

TED   *(confidently)* Four!

RICHARD   No. Okay. Let's try something else… Okay. Okay, okay, okay.
             We've got a pie, okay?

TED   What kind?

RICHARD   Well, whatever kind you want—

TED   Blueberry.

RICHARD   Fine. We want to cut up this blueberry pie into four equal
             pieces, okay?

TED   Sure!

RICHARD   Good. So if we have four equal pieces of pie—

TED   Where is it?

RICHARD   *(beat)* Let's forget about the pie.

TED   That's mean.

RICHARD   Okay, okay, okay, okay. *(holds up a loonie)* What's this?

TED   A dollar.

RICHARD   Yes. Each bar is worth a dollar.

TED   Wow!

RICHARD   Now we already know there are four beats in each bar; that means that each beat is worth…?

TED   Oh! Twenty-five cents.

RICHARD   Yeah… and another way of saying twenty-five cents is…?

TED   Two bits.

RICHARD   And another way of saying two bits is…?

TED   Well, a quarter—

RICHARD   YES!!

> TED *falls back on the keyboard out of shock.*

A QUARTER! A quarter what? A quarter… noo…

BOTH   Nooo… noooo… nooooo…

RICHARD   Note!

TED   Note!

RICHARD   A quarter note!

TED   Okay, I've heard of them.

RICHARD   Four beats in each bar and each beat is worth a quarter note. And that's how we count the piece!

TED   Uh huh. *(beat)* How?

RICHARD   We count... *(points to the music)* one quarter, two quarter, three quarter, four quarter, *(comma sound à la Victor Borge)* new dollar. One quarter, two quarter, three quarter, four quarter. *(comma sound)*

TED   New dollar.

RICHARD   Yes. Now play and count out loud.

At the Tarragon Theatre, 1996.
Photo by Lydia Pawelka.

> TED *plays and counts out loud again but he's counting eighth notes as quarter notes.*

TED   One, two, three, four, *(comma sound)* one, two, three, four, *(comma sound)* one, two, three, four—

RICHARD   No, Teddy. No.

TED   Three bucks!

RICHARD   Teddy, what do we call these notes?

TED   Eee's.

RICHARD   Yes, but we're talking about the time here, Teddy. The time. How much time do we spend on each of those notes?

TED   It seems like forever, Mr. Berkoff.

RICHARD   Okay, you see those notes have little tails on them?

TED   Yeah.

RICHARD   Well that means there are two of those notes with the little tails on them in every quarter note. Which means that each one of those notes with the little tails on them is worth half a quarter. And another way of saying half a quarter is…?

TED   Twelve and a half cents.

RICHARD   And another way of saying twelve and half cents is…?!

TED   I don't know… one bit?

RICHARD   NO!! *(beat)* Yes. One bit. We can actually count the piece that way. Play it, Teddy. Play it. *(He does.)* One bit, two bit, three bit, four bit, *(TED begins to count along.)* one bit, two bit, three bit, four bit. Well, there you go! But the "one," the "two," the "three," and the "four" are more important than the "bits."

TED has a blank look on his face.

They're louder, so we actually go…

TED plays again and they count two bars, emphasizing the numbers—RICHARD stops him.

Okay, okay, okay, but the "one" is the most important and the "two," the "three," and the "four" are less important, so we actually go…

They count two bars out again, emphasizing the "one."

Okay, okay. Okay! But the "three" is also important—it's not as important as the "one" but it's still important, so we actually go…

They count again, emphasizing the one and the three—four bars this time. RICHARD makes his way across to his piano, sits, and plays Beethoven's Sonatina in F badly and with physical contortions. TED makes his way over to RICHARD's piano.

FINGERING

TED

Okay, thank you, Richard. Thank you. Did you practise at all this week?

RICHARD

Yes I did. Half an hour every day, Mr. Morton.

TED

Uh huh. And you included that piece in your practising, did you?

RICHARD

Yeah.

TED

Okay. Let's try it again.

> RICHARD *begins again and* TED *turns to look at what he's doing. He stops* RICHARD *and begins to laugh.*

Hang on a second. What are you doing with your arm there, buddy? What about the fingering?

RICHARD

Fingering?

TED

Didn't your old teacher teach you about fingering?

RICHARD

Well, kind of, I guess.

TED

What the heck did she do?

RICHARD

Well, she usually went upstairs for a cup of tea and a lie down.

TED

All right, all right, all right, all right. Play me an F major scale, buddy, I've seen you do that. *(*RICHARD *does it.)* There you go. That's all there is to it. Now have a gander at the second bar. Tell me what that is without the rest of the piece around it?

RICHARD   It's a going-down F major scale.

TED   So, what do think about that?

RICHARD   You mean you use the same fingering?!

TED   Well sure you do. That's why we make you practise the scales. We don't do it just to be mean. They actually show up in the pieces.

RICHARD   *(plays the passage successfully)* Wow!! *(continues to play)*

TED   There you go. Enjoy yourself. *(TED crosses to his piano.)* See ya next week!

> TED *sits and plays "Our Band Goes To Town" again, but better this time, using the acclaimed Berkoff "one bit" counting method.*

BERKOFF II

RICHARD   Well, that was much better, wasn't it?

TED   Yeah!

RICHARD   That method of counting really helped, didn't it?

TED   Yeah!

RICHARD   You're starting to have some fun now, aren't you?

TED   Yeah!

RICHARD   But you're still not doing it right.

> *RICHARD produces a metronome, turns it on, hands it to TED, and plays and speaks in time.*

Every one bit, two bit, three bit, four bit has to be the same. So, practise with that.

> *RICHARD walks back to his piano. RICHARD, picking up on the tempo, plays the Beethoven Sonatina again, beautifully and right to the end without a single mistake. Delighted, he looks up at TED for approval.*

TED   Well hey! That's a whole heck of a lot better, isn't it?

RICHARD   *(RICHARD nods ecstatically.)* Yeah!

TED   That way of fingering really helped, didn't it?

RICHARD   *(another ecstatic nod)* Yeah!

TED   You're starting to have some fun, huh?

RICHARD   Oh yeah!

TED   Now all you have to do is memorize it. We'll see you next week.

> *TED exits, leaving RICHARD in shock.*

PRACTISE I / SHADOW PLAY

The sound of a metronome is heard (ticking at 138 bpm).
RICHARD *checks to see if anyone notices and tries to sneak off. He is caught. The following offstage voices might be seen in shadow and their voices might be enhanced to caricatures of their parents.*

TED   *(offstage)* RICHARD! I DON'T HEAR ANY PRACTISING!

RICHARD   Do I have to, Mom?

TED   *(offstage)* YOU DO IF YOU WANT YOUR ALLOWANCE.

RICHARD   *(mimics)* You do if you want your allowance. *(to her)* It's not fair! Everybody else is outside playing hockey!

             RICHARD *goes back to his piano and begins to play Mozart's Sonata Facile in C Major.* TED *enters.*

TED   Can't I do it later? *(He sits and plays.)*

RICHARD   I'm just getting a glass of nutritious milk! *(He exits.)*

             TED *plays the same phrase over and over, slowing down and stopping as he realizes that no one is yelling at him. He takes the phone from his bench. The lid slams.*

             (offstage) TEDDY! I DON'T HEAR ANY PRACTISING!

TED   I just stopped for one second!

             TED *resumes playing.* RICHARD *enters and picks up the Sonata from where* TED *left off.*

             I have to go to the bathroom…

> TED *exits. After a few bars,* RICHARD *launches into some boogie-woogie.*

> *(offstage)* RICHARD! THAT'S NOT MOZART!

> RICHARD *switches back to proper practise—he blows a raspberry in Mom's general direction.*

NEITHER IS THAT! *(pause)* RICHARD?

RICHARD   Yeah?

TED   I'M GOING OVER TO THE ADILMANS'. I'LL BE BACK IN FIVE MINUTES.

RICHARD   Okay!

TED   YOU'D BETTER NOT STOP PRACTISING OR THERE WILL BE NO TV TONIGHT!

RICHARD   *(crossing his legs)* I promise.

> *We hear a door slam.* TED *enters and takes over the playing.* RICHARD *wanders offstage.*

Snack time!

TED   *(He picks up the phone and dials as he plays.)* Hey, Jerry. You gonna play hockey? What street? Is she going to be there? *(He laughs.)* She's got big boobs. I should be done in five minutes. *(yells to Dad)* How much longer?

RICHARD   *(offstage)* A GOOD SOLID HALF AN HOUR.

TED   Half an hour!! What clock are you looking at?! *(into the phone)* I'll call you back. *(He runs offstage.)* I started at 5:30, Dad!!

RICHARD enters eating. We hear a door slam and RICH-
ARD *runs to his piano.*

RICHARD   Oh no!

TED   *(offstage)* ALL RIGHT—NO TV, RICHARD!

RICHARD   Noooooooooooo.

RICHARD quickly starts playing. TED *enters.*

TED   Half an hour?!

RICHARD   *(*TED *plays.)* I just stopped for two seconds! I was starving
to death!

TED   *(*RICHARD *plays.)* This is a dictatorship!

RICHARD   *(*TED *plays.) Star Trek* is starting!

TED   *(*RICHARD *plays.)* These are the best years of my life!

*TED and RICHARD trade off playing in smaller and smaller
increments, tagging on a "Shave and a Haircut" ending.
The ticking stops.*

DAD / SON I

TED   All right, Richard! What are you doing?

RICHARD   What do you mean? I'm practising.

TED   You're goofing around again, that's what you're doing. You
think I don't hear the little ending?

He plays "Shave and a Haircut."

That's disrespectful to the music, Richard!!

RICHARD   Dad, will you please stop yelling at me.

TED   *(yelling)* I'm not yelling at you. I'm feeling strongly about what I'm saying! Why can't you practise properly, Richard?

RICHARD   I'm bored.

TED   Oh, you're bored, are you? You're bored with Mozart? The greatest musical genius in the history of mankind bores my son. Well, we're so sorry, Richard. We'll try to do better for you, Richard.

RICHARD   Well this isn't exactly a work of genius. I mean, look what it's called: the Sonata Facile. The easy sonata.

TED   That doesn't mean that it is easy, that means it's supposed to sound easy. Ironically, that is a very difficult thing to do! I remember when I played this one... *(He sits.)*

RICHARD   *(in quiet pain)* Oh God noooo...

TED   ...a little slower than you, but that's up to the individual. *(TED begins to play.)* Right from the beginning—

RICHARD   Dad!

TED   —you have to give the listener the illusion of simplicity.

RICHARD   Dad!

TED   You can't fake your way through these scales—

RICHARD   Earth to Dad!! *(TED stops playing.)* I already have a teacher, you know. I don't want a lesson every single time I practise.

TED   God, you know, you just amaze me sometimes! Do you know how lucky you are to have me helping you?! *(RICHARD slumps.)* When I was your age I didn't have a me to help me. You have the opportunity to be a better player than I ever was and instead you fight me every step of the way!!!

RICHARD   Will you please stop yelling at me?!

TED   All right, that's it!

> *TED clears everything into the bench and puts the stand down.*

I've had it with this, mister. This is a waste of your time and my money! I'll call Mrs. George right now and tell her you're going to quit the piano. How would you like that?

RICHARD   Fine. Go ahead!

TED   I will!

RICHARD   Do it, see if I care!

TED   You're messing with the wrong guy. *(He dials.)* It's ringing. Two rings. Hello, Mrs. George—this is Richard Greenblatt's father, Mr. Greenblatt. Richard has something he'd like to say.

> *He hands the phone to RICHARD, who is horror-stricken.*

RICHARD   Hello, Mrs. George. I think I'm... not quite sure what I'm supposed to be practising this week. *(beat)* Uh hunh. Uh hunh. Oh yeah, the Sonata Facile, I thought so. Okay. See you Saturday. Okay, bye.

TED puts the phone in the bench.

TED   So you don't want to quit?

RICHARD   No.

TED   Well, that's what I thought. *(RICHARD starts to cry.)* Aw, Rich… Okay, Daddy shouldn't have done that… That was not very fair… We won't tell Mom? I'm sorry about that, okay?

TED tries to touch RICHARD, but he moves away.

Okay? Who's my guy?

RICHARD throws himself into his dad's arms and they hug.

We can't keep doing this, Richard. I don't want to go through this every single time you practise. It's just that you're so good, you know, son. That's why Daddy cares so much. And when Daddy cares a lot, Daddy gets loud. Now I want you to make a deal with me, okay?

RICHARD   What kind of deal?

TED   A pact. If you're going to commit to this, seriously commit to classical music, then you're going to practise for one hour every day—

RICHARD   One hour?!

TED   Every day, without exception—

RICHARD   Even on my lesson days?!

TED   Especially on your lesson days.

RICHARD   Don't I get any days off?

TED   All right, statutory holidays.

RICHARD   Oh, gee thanks.

TED   And without ever, ever, ever complaining about it or goofing around during that hour. Outside that hour I think you should goof around—I think it's great and I encourage it—but inside that hour I want you to devote yourself to the practice, perfection, and performance of classical music, from now until you're seventeen years old.

RICHARD   Seventeen?!

TED   Yes.

RICHARD   That's seven more years!

TED   That's how old I was when I quit. And then you can do whatever you like. If you still want to quit right now, to-day, you're free to do so. I'm your father, I'll always love you. I will respect your decision. *(beat)* What do you say? *(He extends a hand.)* Deal?

Just as RICHARD *is about to shake, he stops.*

RICHARD   You gotta make a deal with me too.

TED   Okay, that's fair enough, sir, you name it.

RICHARD   You have to promise to never… ever… ever… ever… prac-tise with me for the rest of your life.

TED   You don't want my help?

RICHARD   No.

TED   Not even when there's a big competition?

RICHARD   No.

TED   'Cause you might regret—

RICHARD   No.

> RICHARD *extends his hand.*

Deal, Dad?

TED   Okay. Okay. Deal.

> *They shake on it and* TED *pulls* RICHARD *closer to him.*

Seven years!

> RICHARD *stares at his hand then exits as* TED *crosses to his piano and sits down to play…*

COMPETITION / DUELLING DUET

> *The Mozart Sonata for One Piano, Four Hands. We hear a doorbell…*

TED   It's open!

> *The doorbell repeats.*

It's open like it was last week… and the week before!

RICHARD enters; they grunt a greeting.

RICHARD   Excuse me, may I have some room please? *(TED shifts on the bench.)* Thank you. And how are you today?

TED   I'm very well, thank you. *Et vous?*

RICHARD   *Très bien, merci,* except for the fact that the bench is too close.

TED   Well I like it this close.

RICHARD   Well I don't.

They move RICHARD's end back two feet.

Merci beaucoup. One, two, three—

TED   Did we, or did we not, agree last week that I would count in the piece?

RICHARD   *(RICHARD gestures for TED to proceed.) Je suis desolé.*

TED   Quite all right. I'm sure you just *oublier.* Two, three, four—

They begin to play but TED stops, reaches over RICHARD, and turns on the metronome.

RICHARD   Oh come on, we don't need that.

TED   *Excusez-moi, Monsieur le Grande Fromage,* this is Mozart that we're practising, not some baby piece. Next week is the eleven and under competition and if we want to stand any chance of winning we have to take it seriously.

RICHARD   A.R.

TED   What's A.R.?

RICHARD   Anal Retentive.

TED   W.R.

RICHARD   What's W.R.?

TED   Without Rhythm. Two, three, four. *(They play and the battle begins...)* Shhh!!

RICHARD   Crescendo.

             RICHARD sticks out his tongue, changing back to a normal face just as TED looks at him. RICHARD sways to the music—TED imitates.

             (yawning) Boring bit. And now I play...

             TED glares. He reaches to turn the page and RICHARD continues to play.

TED   Would you wait for me please?!

             RICHARD stops and points to the metronome.

RICHARD   Well, you've got to stay on the beat!

TED   Well I'm turning the page!

RICHARD   Well, turn it faster!

TED   Well I can't!

RICHARD   One, two—

TED   I count! Two, three, four.

They continue.

TED reaches around the back of RICHARD's head and gently flicks his hair—twice—then gives RICHARD the finger behind his head. RICHARD catches on and whips around... too late to catch TED in the act.

RICHARD hip-checks TED off the bench.

TED pushes the bench out from under RICHARD.

RICHARD pulls his end back so that the bench is parallel to the front of the stage and TED can't sit down.

TED pulls his end around with one foot while continuing to play, leaving RICHARD facing out.

Then they both start pushing back and forth. RICHARD jumps away in an attempt to send TED flying—it doesn't work.

TED stands to turn the page again. RICHARD continues playing. TED slaps away RICHARD's hands a couple of times until he finally blows.

WAIT FOR ME!

Beat. They begin again.

TED hits RICHARD on the head.

RICHARD seeks revenge and takes a swing at TED but TED ducks and RICHARD misses.

RICHARD wets his finger and sticks it in TED's ear.

Agh! What was that?!

At the Tarragon Theatre, 1996.
Photo by Beatrice Campbell.

RICHARD   Woohoo! *(TED smacks RICHARD on the head.)* Ow!

TED   *(RICHARD smacks TED on the head.)* Stop it.

RICHARD   Me stop it?!

TED   Yes.

RICHARD   You started it.

TED   I did not.

RICHARD   You did too.

TED   Did not.

RICHARD   Did too.

TED   Not!

RICHARD   Too!

>   *This shouted exchange continues until the end of the piece.*

BOTH   See you next week.

>   RICHARD *exits and* TED *becomes Ed McFetridge.*

KIWANIS

TED   Thank you very much and good morning once again, ladies and gentlemen, boys and girls. On behalf of the Kiwanis Club, I would like to welcome you all back to the eighty-ninth annual Kiwanis Music Festival, class number four thousand five hundred and sixty-one, Piano Duet—Eleven and Under. My name is Ed McFetridge, from the Kiwanis Club, as most of you probably know by now since it's been my pleasure to have been here since that Monday three weeks ago. This morning's class will consist of... sixty-seven pairs of children, all playing exactly the same piece. It should take about four hours. It is now my pleasure to reintroduce you once again to the adjudicator for this year's proceedings—Dr. *(small pause as he figures it out...)* Boola Noogie.

>   RICHARD *enters and speaks in a thick Hungarian accent.*

RICHARD   Bela Nagy.

TED   *(as he exits)* You should spell it like that.

RICHARD   Tank you very much, Mr. Ed. Good mornink, boys and girls. I am lookink forvard to today. Now, dis duet is very unusual piss, and I vill tell you vhy. At de beginnink, de player on de top plays only von note, den de player on de bottom plays for a long time until de player on de top starts to take his piss. Now, vit duet, it is important to remember dat vonce de players play togeder—de players play togeder! You are team. Is no good if von is taking his piss faster dan de other. Also, please remember vat is title. "In Der Halle des Bergkönigs." "In De Hall of De Mountain Kink," by Edvard Grieg. It is very famous. Now, I vant you to make me feel and smell and taste dis piss. Okay, boys and girls, have goot time. And remember most important ting. Do not take your piss until I ring de bell! Mr. Ed, de first players please. *(He exits.)*

TED   *(offstage)* Thank you, Dr. *(beat)* Noogie. The first contestants this morning are the piano duet team of Ted Disk… Dukes… It's all consonants. And Richard… Greenbladder.

> RICHARD *and* TED *enter shyly. They bow to the audience, move to the piano, do their good luck pinkie twist, and sit and wait. After a short while they look out at the audience. Pause. A bell rings.* TED *plays the first note, they look at each other with congratulatory grins and* RICHARD *begins to play.*
>
> TED *is smiling and looks out at the audience—he slowly realizes how many people are watching him and turns bright red from fear.* RICHARD *looks up as* TED*'s entrance approaches and sees that there is a problem…*

(grabbing RICHARD*'s arm, whispers)* I can't remember it!

RICHARD	*(also whispering)* What do you mean you can't remember it?!
TED	I can't remember anything.
RICHARD	You gotta remember it!
TED	Get the music!
RICHARD	I can't get the music.
TED	If you don't get the music I think I'm going to puke.
RICHARD	Okay. Okay. Don't puke. *(to the adjudicator)* Excuse me, is it okay if we use our music? …Thank you. Mom?! Mom?! Where are you?

> *He spots Mom—an audience member—and runs into the audience to get the music. He runs back to the piano and gives the music to TED.*

I got the music! Play the first note!

> *TED complies with the wrong one—RICHARD starts to play. As TED tries to find the right page, the music falls to the floor and glides under the piano.*

TED	I dropped the music.
RICHARD	*(still playing)* Well pick it up!
TED	You pick it up.
RICHARD	I'm a little busy here!!!

> *TED crawls under the piano to get the music. As he's coming out he bumps his head really hard. He starts to sob, puts the music on the stand, and sits down.*

At the Tarragon Theatre, 1996.
Photo by Lydia Pawelka.

TED   *(He grips RICHARD's arm.)* I can't do it, Rich!!

RICHARD   Oh my God! I'm going to have to play both parts!

               He does and TED interjects with the following…

TED   Why do they make us do this every year?!

RICHARD   Turn the page! Turn the page!!

               He watches RICHARD's hands flying across the keyboard.

TED   You're doing really well!! *(He points.)* F sharp. F sharp.

RICHARD   Shut up! *(RICHARD stops playing.)* Okay. You're going to go
               from here to the end.

TED   I bumped my head.

RICHARD   *(RICHARD begins to strangle TED.)* Six months! Six months we've been working on this piece! Now, you are going to go from there to the end or I'm going to kill you!! One, two, three, four—

> *TED unwillingly complies and they struggle through the finale, both bawling mightily while counting, to the end, at which point RICHARD gets up, bows, and leaves the stage. TED is alone on the bench with his head in his hands...*

TED   Oh God... Oh God... Oh God...

EXAM

> *The centre curtain parts, revealing red backlight.*

RICHARD   *(a voice from hell)* Mr. Dykstra.

TED   Oh God!

RICHARD   Welcome to your Conservatory of Music grade seven piano examination!

TED   Oh God!

> *Snap to reality.*

RICHARD   Now, before hearing your repertoire of pieces and doing some ear testing and some theory, we'll begin with the required technical elements of the examination. As I'm sure you're both well aware of and well prepared for, this will include scales, arpeggios, chords, and such in a key of my choosing. And the special key that I have chosen for you today is... *(TED crosses his fingers.)* C sharp!

TED   Shit!

RICHARD   I'm sorry, Mr. Dykstra... did you say something?

TED   Sharp?

RICHARD   Yes. Sharp. We'll begin with the C sharp major scale, parallel hands, four octaves, sixteenth notes and legato, when you are ready.

> TED *performs the scale well and quietly thanks God for his help.*

Good. The formula pattern, please. *(TED aces it.)* Very good. The relative minor scale, please. *(TED begins but RICHARD stops him.)* One moment. One moment, Mr. Dykstra. You're playing the harmonic minor.

TED   Yes?

RICHARD   How many minor scales are there, young man?

TED   Three.

RICHARD   And they are?

TED   Harmonic, melodic, and regular, I mean natural! Regular?!

RICHARD   So, if I ask you for the relative minor scale of a given major key, the scale that I want has the same accidentals as its relative major, which would be?

TED   Oh. Just the natural minor scale?

RICHARD   Of course.

TED   You want me to play the natural minor scale first?

RICHARD   Absolutely.

TED   Okay.

RICHARD   Didn't your teacher explain this to you?

TED   I'm sure he must have.

RICHARD   Proceed.

> *TED plays well until the very last chord.*

An interesting variation. The C sharp major arpeggio, please.

> *TED plays it well.*

Relative minor arpeggio… in tenths.

TED   Sorry?

RICHARD   The relative minor arpeggio in tenths.

TED   In tenths?

RICHARD   Yes.

TED   You mean a tenth apart?

RICHARD   Yes.

TED   Is that in the syllabus, sir?

RICHARD   I wrote the syllabus.

TED   Oh you're that guy!

> *He sort of attempts the arpeggio.* RICHARD *writes while "tsking."*

RICHARD   The C sharp major arpeggio again, please. Contrary motion this time.

TED   (TED *looks very uncomfortable.*) Contrary motion arpeggio? (RICHARD *nods.*) So… the one hand would go the one way and the other hand would…

> RICHARD *nods.* TED *looks at the keyboard.*

Oooh, I don't think so, sir!

RICHARD   Mr. Dykstra, did you practise those at all?

TED   No, sir, I did not.

RICHARD   And why not?

TED   I did not know I had to, sir.

RICHARD   Who is your teacher, young man?

TED   Mr. Berkoff.

RICHARD   Ah. "One-bit-two-bit-three-bit" Berkoff. Mr. Dykstra, I must tell you how very disappointed I am with how under-prepared you are in this area.

TED   Well, that would make two of us.

RICHARD   However, I am not going to blame you. Do you know that I can tell by the time a student has played one scale whether or not they have talent?

TED   Oh boy.

RICHARD   You, Mr. Dykstra, you have talent.

TED   Oh boy.

RICHARD   What you do not have is a good teacher. And what you will
not get on this examination… is a high mark. You are on
the verge of graduating to a whole new level with your music. Soon you will be playing pieces by the masters, which
will excite and challenge you in ways you've never dreamed.
(TED sighs.) Now, my advice to you is that after this examination is over, you have a long chat with your parents and
seriously consider changing teachers.

TED   You mean just dumping Mr. Berkoff?

RICHARD   Basically yes.

TED   I've been with Mr. Berkoff my whole life. I like Mr. Berkoff.

RICHARD   And I like him too, but he can't help you anymore. Mr. Berkoff
is fine for beginners or young people who are not serious
about playing well. *(beat)* Mr. Dykstra, are you serious about
playing well?

TED   Yes.

RICHARD   Good. Now, I can give you the names of some excellent teachers or, who knows, maybe I'll even take you on myself. *(TED
laughs nervously.)* However, if you would like to achieve ex-
cellence, you will "dump" Mr. Berkoff and as soon as possible.
(beat) Now, let's move on to some ear testing, shall we?

    *Shift to TED as the instructor. TED stands and plays a C
    major chord.*

TED   Sing this back to me. *(He plays a short melody; RICHARD
looks down.)* Without looking at the keyboard.

RICHARD sings back the melody.

Shift to RICHARD as the instructor. RICHARD stands and plays a D minor chord.

RICHARD   Clap this back to me. *(TED begins to clap and stomp.)* Not with your feet, just with your hands.

Shift to TED as the instructor. TED stands and plays an E minor chord.

TED   What is the relative major of E minor? *(RICHARD looks down.)* No looking at the keyboard!

RICHARD   *(to himself)* Baruch atah Adonai... G major!

Shift to RICHARD as the instructor. He stands and plays an F minor chord.

Sing a perfect fifth above this note.

He plays a G and TED begins to hum the scale.

Not the notes in between, just the note! *(TED sings the note.)*

Shift to TED as the instructor. He stands and plays an A minor chord.

TED   What is the sub-dominant of A? *(RICHARD counts on his fingers.)* No counting! *(RICHARD looks down.)* No looking at the keyboard!!

RICHARD   D!

Shift to RICHARD as the instructor. RICHARD stands and plays a G major chord with a B bass.

How many flats are there in C flat major?

TED   Seven.

RICHARD   And they are?

TED   Battle Ends And Down Goes Charles' Father.

RICHARD   *(overtop of TED)* NO!! Just the letters!!

TED   B-E-A-D-G-C's father—F.

> *Shift to TED as the instructor. TED stands and plays a C major chord.*

TED   Name Beethoven's nephew.

RICHARD   Name Beethoven's *nephew*?

TED   Name Beethoven's nephew. *(RICHARD looks down.)* Without looking at the keyboard!!

> *TED picks up the clipboard.*

Stand over there.

> *RICHARD crosses to the spotlight downstage centre.*

Beethoven's nephew?

RICHARD   *(a wild guess)* Uh… Fred?

TED   Correct. *(RICHARD, amazed, grins.)* Johann Sebastian Bach dates?

RICHARD   1685 to 1750.

TED   Mozart dates?

RICHARD   1756 to 1791.

TED   Beethoven dates?

RICHARD   1770 to 1827.

TED   Three of Bach's offspring who became composers?

RICHARD   Carl Philipp Emanuel, Johann Christian, and... Fred?

TED   Nice try. Name a Finnish composer.

RICHARD   Sebelius.

TED   Norwegian composer?

RICHARD   Grieg.

TED   Polish composer?

RICHARD   Chopin.

TED   Hungarian composer?

RICHARD   Bartók.

TED   Italian composer?

RICHARD   Vivaldi.

TED   American composer?

RICHARD   Ives.

TED   German composer?

RICHARD   Bach.

TED   *(quickly)* Another one?

RICHARD   Beethoven.

TED   Another one?

RICHARD   Handel.

TED   Another one?

RICHARD   Strauss.

TED   Another one?

RICHARD   Brahms.

TED   Russian composer?

RICHARD   Rimsky-Korsakov.

TED   *(quickly)* Another one?

RICHARD   Stravinsky.

TED   Another one?

RICHARD   Shostakovich.

TED   Another one?

RICHARD   Tchaikovsky.

TED   Another one?

RICHARD   Khachaturian.

>*Beat.* RICHARD *is quite pleased with himself.*

TED   Canadian composer? *(big blank from* RICHARD*)* Canadian
             composer? *(blank)* What's your nationality, young man?

RICHARD   Canadian.

TED   And you don't know a single Canadian composer... well,
             well.

RICHARD   Do you?

TED   That's hardly the point.

RICHARD   Shaffer!

TED   First name?

RICHARD   Paul.

TED   That'll do.

RICHARD   Yes!

TED   Allegro?

RICHARD   A fast-ish tempo.

TED   Adagio?

RICHARD   A slow-ish tempo.

TED   Allegretto.

RICHARD   A little allegro...

>TED *stops and looks at* RICHARD.

TED   Andante?

RICHARD   A moderate walking pace.

TED   Lento?

RICHARD   Slow.

TED   Presto?

RICHARD   Fast.

TED   Molto con brio.

RICHARD   Much with brio, bubbly like the Italian soft drink…

              TED stops again to look at him.

TED   Ritardando?

RICHARD   Getting slower.

TED   Crescendo?

RICHARD   Getting louder.

TED   Rallentando?

RICHARD   Held back.

TED   Rubato?

RICHARD   In robbed time.

TED   Tenuto?

RICHARD   Held.

TED   Ornamente?

RICHARD   Ornamentally.

TED   Tranquillemente?

RICHARD   Tranquilly.

TED   Appoggiatura?

RICHARD   It's a little grace note.

TED   Acatchitura?

RICHARD   Gezundheit.

TED   Thank you.

RICHARD   You're welcome. *(They share a puzzled look.)*

TED   Mezzo forte?

RICHARD   Medium loud.

TED   Forte?

RICHARD   Loud.

TED   Fortissimo?

RICHARD   Very loud.

TED   Fortississimo?

RICHARD   Very, very loud.

TED   Fortissississimo?

RICHARD   Very, very, very, loud.

TED   Fortississississississi—

RICHARD   *(counting)* Very, very, very, very—

TED   Staccato?!

RICHARD   Off.

TED   Legato?

RICHARD   Smooth.

TED   Agitato?

TED throws the clipboard away.

RICHARD   Agitatedly.

TED   Appassionato!!

RICHARD   PASSIONATELY!!

TED   MAESTOSO!!

RICHARD   MAJESTICALLY!!

TED   POLONAISE!!

RICHARD   IN THE POLISH WAY!!

TED   HOLLANDAISE!!

RICHARD   IN THE DUTCH WAY!!

TED   MAYONNAISE!!

RICHARD   IN THE CLUB SANDWICH!!

TED   BAGATELLE!!

RICHARD   IT'S A LITTLE BAGEL!!

TED   ÉTUDE!!!

RICHARD   IT'S WHAT CAESAR SAID TO BRUTUS!!!

They look at their hands and begin to move away from each other.

BOTH   AAAAHHHHHHHHHH!!!

When they reach the edge of the stage the lights change and they turn to face each other, biting their nails.

At the Tarragon Theatre, 1996.
Photo by Beatrice Campbell.

NERDS

RICHARD   Hi, Teddy.

TED   Hi, Ricky.

BOTH   How ya doin'? Fine. I haven't seen you since last year. *(nerdy laugh)*

RICHARD   So have you finished signing up for the competition yet?

TED   Yup.

RICHARD   Me too. So, what classes are you entered in this year?

TED   Oh boy... there's the Bach Twelve-and-Under Two Part Inventions.

RICHARD   Oh really? Me too. *(They both laugh nerdily.)* Which one are you playing?

TED   C major.

RICHARD   Oh yeah. *(They both sing a bar or two.)*

TED   You?

RICHARD   F major.

TED   Oh sure... *(They both sing a bit.)* What else?

RICHARD   Twelve-and-Under Chopin Waltzes.

TED   Really? Me too. *(They laugh.)* Which one?

RICHARD   Number ten. *(They sing it.)* You?

TED   Number three.

RICHARD   Oh yeah. *(They sing it.)*

TED   Haydn Sonata?

RICHARD   No, actually.

TED   No?

RICHARD   No.

TED   No?

RICHARD   No.

TED   Oh.

RICHARD   My teacher says that the sonata they chose for the competi-
           tion this year is not one of Haydn's better sonatas. I'm doing
           Contemporary Music instead.

TED   Oh really. I prefer music that has a melody. *(They both sniff.)*
           Oh. I'm also in the Sixteen-and-Under Concerto Class.

RICHARD   The Bach D Minor?

TED   The Bach D Minor, yup.

RICHARD   Oh really?

TED   Yeah.

RICHARD   *(beat)* Me too.

TED   Oh really? *(Pause, then they both laugh warily.)* Have you
           memorized it yet?

RICHARD   Pretty much. Listen, how fast are you playing it?

TED   Oh I don't know…a hundred and four, hundred and eight BPMS. You?

RICHARD   A hundred and twelve.

TED   Well sure, I tried it that fast but my teacher says it's too fast. *(They both sniff.)*

RICHARD   Well, one of us is bound to win.

TED   One of us always does.

RICHARD   *(with horror)* Except for last year.

TED   *(with the same horror)* Oh yeah… that little eight-year-old Chinese girl.

BOTH   Thank God she moved away.

TED   Well, good luck to you.

RICHARD   *(They shake hands.)* Yeah, you too.

TED   And I really mean that.

RICHARD   You know… I don't care if I don't win—

BOTH   —as long as I do my best.

TED   And as long as you don't do your best. *(TED laughs.)* That's a good one. *(TED laughs.)* Well. Happy practising.

RICHARD   Contradiction in terms. *(They both laugh.)*

BOTH   That's a good one.

They both sniff and turn away biting their nails.

They look back at one another and then quickly run to their pianos to get the Bach D Minor out of their benches. They are now in their own separate worlds.

TED   I can't believe he's in that class.

RICHARD   Oh my God, I better get to work.

TED   The only reason I signed up for the Bach D Minor was because I didn't think he would be in it.

            RICHARD begins to practise as TED flips through the music.

            It's sixty-seven pages long!! *(TED plays.)*

RICHARD   Oh yeah! Like someone could actually play this?! *(RICHARD plays.)*

TED   Houston, we have a problem. *(TED plays.)*

RICHARD   *(looking to the heavens)* Thanks a lot, Mr. Bach!

BOTH   HELP!!

            And they play a final crashing chord together—blackout.

            Interval.

ACT II

LESSONS II

In the dark we hear TED *playing Chopin's Prelude in D Flat Major.*

The lights come up slowly. After about two minutes RICHARD *enters and begins his instruction...*

RICHARD   Much better, Teddy. But... she's still dreaming... And here she takes a deep breath... *(He does.)* And now she's going to wake up! *(He does.)* And she checks on her baby. Shhh, we don't want to wake the baby, do we?

TED   *(under his breath)* Nooo...

RICHARD   But the baby is fine. And so... she falls back... to sleep. *(The piece ends.)* Oh. Now isn't that so much better, Teddy?

> TED *stands, looks at* RICHARD, *is about to say something but can't, and exits.*

> RICHARD *sits to his piano and plays "Leyenda" by Albéniz.*

> *After about a minute he begins to hunch over the keyboard—*TED *enters and stands behind* RICHARD. *He takes*

ten or twelve hairs from the crown of RICHARD's *head between his thumb and forefinger, pulling* RICHARD *up like a marionette into a more proper position.* TED *lets go and* RICHARD *hunches over again, playing all the while.* TED *straightens him again.* RICHARD *finishes a passage.*

TED   Don't sit in it. Go right through.

> RICHARD *continues. He begins to moan—*TED *puts his hand over* RICHARD's *mouth.*

> RICHARD *lowers himself to the keyboard once again.* TED *crosses to his piano.*

Sit up, Richard! You're not Glenn Gould!!

> RICHARD *plays the final chord of the piece and* TED *sits down at his piano.*

> TED *plays the end of Chopin's Rondo for Two Pianos, Four Hands.* RICHARD *crosses over to* TED. RICHARD *speaks with a French accent.*

RICHARD   *Mais Théodore! Qu'est-ce que tu fais?*

TED   What do you mean?

RICHARD   Why do you play these arpeggios *avec une main*… with one hand?

TED   Well, that's how it's written, M. Franck.

RICHARD   And where does it say that?

TED   Well… it doesn't exactly say that, but it doesn't say not to play it with one hand.

RICHARD *Écoutes, Théodore!* There is only one thing that matters when you play the piano… the sound. When you play the arpeggios with one hand, you cannot play them beautifully, all you can do is *show* you can play them with one hand.

TED My old teacher told me expressly to play arpeggios with one hand.

RICHARD And who is this?

TED Mr. Scarlatti.

RICHARD *L'italien?*

TED Yeah.

RICHARD *Oh cochon!! Écoutes, Théodore,* do not listen to this macho macho man. The piano is like a woman. *(TED grins.)* You like the women, *non? Ah oui, Théodore,* I can see you do.

TED M. Franck…

RICHARD And when you make love to a woman… do you use only one hand?

TED I don't know.

RICHARD Theodore, you do not. You make love to her with every part of your body.

TED Okay.

RICHARD You make love to her with your eyes, you make love to her with your lips, you make love to her with your fingertips— of both hands. You caress her. *(He plays the arpeggio.)* You stroke her, *(He plays the arpeggio.)* and you will make the

most beautiful music together. Play, Theodore. Play the arpeggios with both hands.

> TED *plays the arpeggios with both hands.*

TED   Oohhhhh YEAH!

> RICHARD *sits at his piano and plays Schumann's*
> *Fantasiestücke No. 2.* TED *marches over and begins bark-*
> *ing instructions.* TED *speaks with a German accent.*

Tempo! Tempo! *(He claps.)* Where is the melody? Those are
sixteenth notes, *ja??!*

RICHARD   Yeah!

TED   Separate them! Lift *und* separate! Lift me up! Sing!

> *A bewildered* RICHARD *starts singing loudly as he plays.*

Not you sing, the MUSIC SING!! I want you to make me feel
like I've never been loved—

> RICHARD *stops playing and looks at him.*

Never mind!

> TED *sits at* RICHARD's *piano and plays a portion of*
> *Beethoven's Pathétique Sonata.*

> RICHARD *picks up* TED's *right hand and shakes it.* TED
> *continues playing.* RICHARD *picks up* TED's *left hand,*
> *shakes it, slaps it to loosen it, and pats* TED *on the back.*
> TED *continues nervously waiting for the next time.* RICH-
> ARD *reaches for* TED's *right hand and* TED *leaps up...*

TED   DON'T TOUCH ME!!!

> RICHARD *sits at his piano and plays the same passage from the Chopin Rondo except with two hands.* TED *picks up his pile of music books and walks slowly to downstage centre, drops the books, and lies down.* RICHARD *finishes.* TED *speaks with an Italian accent.*

TED   Ricky, Ricky… what you do, enhh?

RICHARD   What do you mean, Mr. Scarlatti?

TED   Why do play those arpeggios with-a two hand?

RICHARD   I don't know, I just thought it'd be easier. That's okay, isn't it?

TED   No, it's not okay. Where does it say in-a da music, "Hey, use-a two hand here, it's-a easier?!" Enhh? Where does it say that?

RICHARD   Well, it doesn't actually say that, but it doesn't say not to play them with two hands either.

TED   Ricardo, Ricardo. You gonna go to the music camp this summer, eh?

RICHARD   Yeah.

TED   You gonna be one of two hundred young people from around the world?

RICHARD   Yeah.

TED   You know… *(getting up)* You know who's gonna be there?

RICHARD   Yeah. Some of the best kids and teachers from around the world. From China, Russia, all over Canada—

TED   Sure, sure. Never mind. There's gonna be chicks! You like-a the chicks?

RICHARD   Well, I don't get out much.

TED   But you like-a the chicks?!

RICHARD   Oh yeah!

TED   That's a good boy. And the chicks, you think they like-a the guy with the crossover fou-fou Liberace hands—enh? With the diamond ring and the poodle and the TV show, enh? No! They like-a the MAN. They like-a the real man! They like-a the man who play the arpeggio with-a one hand. Say, "Hey, I'm no sissy boy." *(He plays the arpeggio with one hand.)* I'm a man. I'm a real man!

RICHARD   Wow!

TED   You wanna have a good time this summer?

RICHARD   Oh yeah.

TED   You want to get-a the chicks?

RICHARD   Oh yeah!

TED   Then you listen to Mr. Scarlatti. *(He whistles.)* Play the arpeggio always with-a one hand.

> *TED crosses to his piano. RICHARD plays an arpeggio, tries to be debonair.*

RICHARD   Hi there! My name's Richard—what's yours? *(plays)* I'm from Montreal—where are you from? *(plays)* Did you notice that I play my arpeggios *(like Mr. S.)* with-a one hand?!

> *TED and RICHARD play the end of the Chopin together.*

DAD / SON II

*TED plays the second movement of Beethoven's Pathétique
Sonata as RICHARD listens. RICHARD flicks a switch. Light
floods into the room.*

RICHARD   Ted.

TED   Dad.

RICHARD   You're playing very beautifully these days, son.

TED   Thanks.

RICHARD   You know, when that adjudicator said that you were the re-
incarnation of Chopin, it made me very proud.

TED   Thanks, Dad, that means a lot to me.

RICHARD   Ted, I was wondering if I could have a word with you.

TED   Can this wait?

RICHARD   No, I'm sorry, it can't wait.

RICHARD takes TED's music off the stand.

TED   What are you doing? Don't!

RICHARD   Ted, I'm a little concerned about you.

TED   Concerned what?!

RICHARD   Well, you're spending all your time cooped up in here practising the piano. You don't have much of a social life, you
have very few friends…

On stage at the Panasonic Theatre, Toronto, during Ted and Richard's farewell tour, 2011. *Photo by Rick O'Brien.*

TED   What are you talking about?! That's not even true. What about Jonathan, my duet partner? Or the Monday night ear-training parties at Mr. Geizeking's?

RICHARD   Yeah, Ted. I'm talking about non-music-related friends. Do you have any non-music-related friends?

TED   Why?

RICHARD   Because there is a world beyond the piano. What about sports, huh? You used to love playing hockey and baseball...

TED   Dad, I hurt my fingers. I couldn't practise for two weeks! I almost missed the festival!

RICHARD   Well, there must be one sport that won't hurt your little fingers?!

TED   Well, I don't like Ping-Pong, what do you want me to do?

RICHARD   Ted, you gotta get outside more. When was the last time you were outside in the sun?

TED   This morning when I went to my lesson.

RICHARD   I'm talking about a non-music-related activity; when was the last time you even took part in a non-music-related activity?

TED   Why?

RICHARD   Because you're becoming obsessive. I don't think it's healthy—

> RICHARD *plays "Chopsticks"*—TED *interrupts by placing his hands on the strings.*

TED   Dad! Get to the point, okay. I'm busy here.

RICHARD   All right. The point is your grades are slipping.

TED   That's the point of this?! We're going to do this now?!

RICHARD   You bet your little cotton socks we are.

TED   I'm in the middle of—

RICHARD   Ted, you used to be an honours student, now you're barely passing.

TED   Sixty-five is not "barely passing," for starters!

RICHARD   It is in my books. Now the only reason you're not still getting eighties is because you're spending all your time at the piano.

TED   That's what it takes at this stage of the game, Dad.

RICHARD   Well let me remind you what it takes to get into a good university at this stage of the game…

TED   I don't need to be reminded…

Then simultaneously…

RICHARD   Ted, it takes two to three hours a day of homework… it takes serious studying at exam time and, Ted, those aptitude tests—

TED   …what it takes to get into a good university, Dad! Please help me Lord! Excuse me…

TED   Excuse me! *(beat)* I'm not going to go to university.

RICHARD   *(laughs)* Ted, what are you talking about?

TED   I don't need high marks in high school, Dad.

RICHARD   Says who?

TED   Says Mr. Geizeking, for one.

RICHARD   Mr. Geizeking said that?

TED   Mr. Geizeking said that.

RICHARD   What else did Mr. Geizeking say?

TED   He said even high school is basically non-essential.

RICHARD   Oh, he did, did he?

TED   I'm going to be a professional musician, not a brain surgeon.

RICHARD   Whoa, whoa, whoa, hold on a second here. When was this decision made?

TED   A long time ago.

RICHARD   Well you can't make a decision like that just like that.

TED   I can so.

RICHARD   You cannot.

TED   I can so!

RICHARD   You cannot!

TED   It's my life!

RICHARD   Not yet it isn't!

TED   Mr. Geizeking said Juilliard will accept anyone if they're good enough regardless of their academic background.

RICHARD   Well Mr. Geizeking is not your father, I am.

TED   Don't I know it.

RICHARD   *(beat)* All right. All right, you want to try to become a professional musician—

TED   You see, Dad, right there! I don't want to *try* to become anything, I'm going to *be* a professional musician. That's what I'm going to do.

RICHARD   Fine. Then you're going to do it properly. You'll get into a top-notch university—

TED   I highly doubt it.

RICHARD   —and then you'll get a degree so that you'll have something to fall back on.

TED   I don't want anything to fall back on.

RICHARD   Ted. The music business is highly competitive. I mean, what
           happens if you're not good enough to make it? What are you
           going to do—work in a piano bar? *(He laughs.)*

TED   I don't know. What would you like me to do, Dad? You want
           me to base my whole life's plan on the fact that you think
           I'm going to fail at the one thing that I really love and that
           I'm really good at? Is that what you want me to do? *(beat)*
           Then I'd end up just like you.

RICHARD   I'm a failure?

TED   I didn't mean it like that—

RICHARD   I just started with nothing—

TED   I know you did, Dad—

           Then simultaneously…

RICHARD	TED
—and I built up a business to the point where I've been able to provide for my family all these years, that's all. To pay for the best and the most expensive piano teacher in this city—Mr. Geizeking.	—it's just that you're always saying that you never got to do what you wanted to do and you had to give everything up so that you could give us all the things you never had, and that's not something that I'm interested— You don't listen to what I say anyway!

RICHARD   To buy you a goddamned grand piano!

TED   Well you're my father, that's your job!

RICHARD   *(beat)* You live in my house.

TED   Oh God.

RICHARD   You eat the food I buy. You live the privileged life that I've—

TED   Privileged?! Oh this is the privileged life, is it?

RICHARD   *(pause)* Yes. Yes it is. You spoiled brat. *(beat)* Now, you are
           going to get an eighty percent average, you're going to go
           to a good university that is...

TED   *(as RICHARD continues over top)* I don't have to go to university
           if I don't want to—

RICHARD   ...mutually agreed upon by the both of us, or else there will
           be no more music in this house. Do you understand me,
           Ted? No lessons. No Mr. Geizeking and his Monday night
           ear-training parties. No piano at all. I'll sell the goddamned
           thing. *(TED starts to speak but RICHARD cuts him off)* That's
           it! End of discussion! Case closed.

           *RICHARD slowly crosses to his piano, unhappy with how
           that all went.*

PRACTISE II / DIVERSIONS

> TED *begins to angrily practise the Mephisto Waltz by Franz Liszt. He stops.*

TED   Oh yeah. Me and whose army?

> RICHARD *begins to practise the Chopin's Ballade No. 2 in F Major. He stops playing and looks to the heavens.*

RICHARD   Thanks a lot, Mr. Chopin!

TED   *(continues with the Mephisto Waltz)* Help me, Rhonda.

RICHARD   *(continues with Chopin Ballade)* Aaarrgh!!

> *He stops playing and picks up the music.*

At the Great Canadian Theatre Company, Ottawa,
during the first Canadian tour, 1996.
Photo by Beatrice Campbell.

How are you supposed to make your fingers do that?!

> TED *continues with the Mephisto Waltz—then hurts his hand and begins banging the piano. He stops on a chord... repeats it five more times, and breaks into a pop song based on that chord.*

> RICHARD *continues with his practising.*

Come on!

> *He plays some more then stops and looks at his hand.*

Come on!

> *He continues and suddenly recognizes a melody...* RICHARD *plays a song based on that melody.*

> TED *and* RICHARD *play through a selection of several pop tunes.*

> *Finally,* TED *is playing a '50s rock-and-roll solo, including the trademark kicking back the bench and playing while standing.* RICHARD *crosses over to* TED *and puts his hand on the piano...*

CONSERVATORY / HITTING THE WALL

…TED falls to the ground in shock.

RICHARD   What *are* you doing?

TED   I was just practising. While I was waiting for you. And I started to fool around a little bit.

RICHARD   For your information, that kind of fooling around is not allowed anywhere in this conservatory. What we do here is practise, perfect, and perform music. Serious music.

TED   I know that, sir. I was aware of the rules and I don't have an excuse. I'm terribly embarrassed at the moment and I can only promise you that it will not happen again.

RICHARD   *(beat)* Very well. This is the second half of your audition into the conservatory, yesterday's recital being the first. Today what we'll do is we'll chat for a bit. I'll test your ear and your rhythm, and then I'll give you some feedback from your recital yesterday, okay?

TED   Cool.

RICHARD   *(rolling his eyes)* Let's start with why you want to become a classi—*do* you want to become a classical musician?

TED   Yes, sir, of course I do.

RICHARD   Why?

TED   Well, I think it's what I do best. A lot of people have encouraged me in this direction; I think it's what I want to do with my life.

RICHARD   You think?

TED   No, I mean I know. I see what you're trying to do here, sir.

RICHARD   What am I trying to do here?

TED   Trying to test my confidence level.

RICHARD   I don't think you have a problem in that area. And what kind of music do you like best?

TED   Composers?

RICHARD   Okay.

TED   Well I'd have to say that the top three for me without a doubt are Bach, Beethoven, and Mozart.

RICHARD   And why are they your "top three"?

TED   There's a lot of reasons. I think each one of those three guys changed totally what came before, they didn't follow anyone else, they broke new ground, they inspire me personally.

RICHARD   They inspire me as well.

TED   Cool. *(Another eye roll from RICHARD.)*

RICHARD   And where do you see yourself in say, ten years, as a classical pianist?

TED   Well hopefully I'll be touring. Soloist. Soloist.

RICHARD   And if I were to say to you that you're not good enough to be a soloist? That the best you could hope for is to be an accompanist, or a teacher? Would that change your mind about wanting to come here?

TED   *(beat)* No, sir. I see what you're trying to do here; but I'm not afraid, I know I can do it.

RICHARD   Very well. Let's move on to some ear testing, shall we?

TED   Cool.

RICHARD   I'll play some intervals and you tell me what they are, please. Turn around, Mr. Dykstra—you can see the hammers from there.

> *TED reacts with disbelief and turns away. RICHARD proceeds to play a series of intervals—TED gets them right.*

TED   *(RICHARD plays.)* Diminished fifth. *(RICHARD plays.)* Minor sixth. *(RICHARD plays.)* Major seventh. *(RICHARD plays.)* Minor ninth.

RICHARD   Yes. What's this chord? *(RICHARD plays.)*

TED   Augmented triad. *(RICHARD plays.)* Diminished.

RICHARD   Diminished what?

TED   Diminished seventh. *(RICHARD plays a major seven.)* That's a major seventh chord. *(RICHARD then plays a minor major seventh.)*

TED   That's... a good one. Could you play that again, please? *(RICHARD repeats the chord.)* Oh! Thingy! It's a minor chord with a major seventh on top.

RICHARD   We call that a minor major seventh chord. I'm going to clap four and I want you to clap three against it.

TED   Four against three? I can do that one myself. It's just a little
               thing that I do! *(He demonstrates.)* Four with the left hand…
               three with the right hand.

RICHARD   Very impressive.

TED   Thank you, sir.

RICHARD   I'd like you to play the A flat Schubert Impromptu that you
               played at yesterday's recital. Can you take it from the middle
               of the recapitulation where the left hand has the melody?
               Do you know where I'm talking about?

TED   No problemo.

RICHARD   *(closing his eyes in pain)* Whenever you're ready, Mr. Dykstra.

               TED *plays. When he finishes, he waits for* RICHARD *to
               speak.*

               You're very talented.

TED   Thank you, sir.

RICHARD   Unfortunately, it's wasted. Play it again from the beginning
               for me, please. I'd like you to take it significantly slower and
               no sustaining pedal.

TED   Is that how you think it should go, sir?

RICHARD   That's how I've asked you to play it.

TED   No pedal? *(*TED *begins to play.)*

RICHARD   Mr. Dykstra. Significantly slower. *(*TED *tries to play it slowly.
               He can't.)*

TED   Sorry. I just have to do this for one second.

             He plays it at speed then tries once again to slow it down.

RICHARD   Make it even, please. *(TED continues.)* Mr. Dykstra. Pianissimo
             as written. *(TED puts his foot on the soft pedal.)* Without the
             aid of the una corda pedal.

             TED continues unsuccessfully. Finally RICHARD intervenes.

             You see? *(TED nods.)* You're cheating the phrase. You're
             faking it because you don't have the discipline, the com-
             mitment, or the desire to perfect it. I've read your records;
             you've managed to impress a lot of adjudicators at the pro-
             vincial finals but frankly, Mr. Dykstra, you don't impress
             me. I find you to be a lazy, arrogant teenager who practis-
             es—what?—an hour and a half, two hours a day? There are
             hundreds of talented young people out there. I have thir-
             teen-year-old students who could play circles around you.
             They have no more talent—there's only one difference be-
             tween them and you. They *work. (beat)* How dare you. How
             dare you waste your talent! Maybe, *maybe*—if you practise
             for five hours a day for two years—*maybe* you will qualify
             to enter into this program. But frankly, Mr. Dykstra, I don't
             believe you have it in you. Here. Here's a quarter. Go and
             call your piano teacher, tell him that you will never ever be
             a classical pianist. Or you can use it to phone the conser-
             vatory to withdraw your application. *(beat)* Good day, Mr.
             Dykstra.

             *RICHARD returns to his piano and sits. TED is left alone,
             devastated. At length, he stands.*

JAZZ FACULTY

TED   Good morning. Mr. Greenblatt?

RICHARD   Hi.

TED   Can I call you Rich?

RICHARD   Sure.

TED   Hey, Rich. Paul Thelon.

RICHARD   Mr. Thelon.

TED   Call me Paul. Welcome to the jazz faculty—the Jazz "Factory"
            as the kids like to call it. This is nothing to worry about, just
            a little "get to know ya," talk about your background, try out
            your rhythm, test your ears, that kind of thing. We like to
            weed before we garden. So I understand you've got a clas-
            sical background. That's kinda weird, you want to tell me
            something about it?

RICHARD   Sure. I've been studying classically for about ten years but, I
            don't know, recently I feel like I've hit a dead end. I've been
            thinking of giving up my classical training.

TED   Okay. Good idea.

RICHARD   In the last few years I've been in some rock groups. Um…
            progressive rock, celtic rock, klezmer rock, that kind of
            thing. I've been accompanying a lot of dance classes.

TED   Gross.

RICHARD   Really! And I've been writing a fair amount of my own stuff.

TED   Now we're talking. Some jazz?

RICHARD   Well, I guess not what you'd call traditional jazz or, I don't know, fusion. I've been doing a lot of blues.

TED   Blues?

RICHARD   The granddaddy of them all! I've been doing quite a study on the blues, actually. I've been reading a lot of books.

TED   Books on the blues?

RICHARD   Yeah. Do you know *Blues Fell This Morning* by Paul Oliver?

TED   No, I can't say that I do, Rich.

RICHARD   Wow. It is a great book. You've gotta read it, Paul.

TED   Okey doke. What's your favourite kind of music?

RICHARD   I really like all kinds.

TED   Jazz. Favourite kind of jazz?

RICHARD   I really like all kinds. *(He laughs. The joke falls flat.)* Uh, Oscar Peterson, of course. Art Tatum—wow! Chick, and Herbie…

TED   Why do you want become a jazz musician, Rich?

RICHARD   Well I feel like I've got jazz in my soul. If you can say that we white guys have soul.

TED   In music, being "white" is not just about skin colour.

RICHARD   Far out, right on, cool, I hear ya.

TED	Okay. I think I've learned a little bit about you. Let's give the ears a shake, shall we? You want to stand over there.

TED plays a series of intervals.

RICHARD	Augmented fourth. *(TED plays.)* Augmented fifth. *(TED plays.)* Minor ninth. *(TED plays.)* Major seventh. *(TED plays a chord this time.)* Augmented triad. *(TED plays a diminished seventh.)* Diminished.

TED	Diminished what?

RICHARD	Diminished seven.

TED plays a minor major seven, RICHARD gets it right. Then TED plays a "complicated" jazz chord.

RICHARD	Sorry. Could you play that one again?

He plays it again. RICHARD starts to hum and guess...

TED	We won't worry about that one. Let me hear you play five against four—five with your right hand, four with your left hand.

RICHARD	*Five* on four?

TED	Uh hunh.

RICHARD attempts to bang out five on four. He stops and looks at TED. Beat.

I was kinda hoping for a tune there. Can you play me something, Rich?

RICHARD	Sure, what?

TED   Well, call me nutty, but how about some jazz? Do you know
            any standards?

RICHARD   "My Funny Valentine"?

TED   Sure, I'd love to hear your crack at "Valentine." Just one time
            through if you don't mind.

            RICHARD plays his version of "My Funny Valentine."

I don't know how to tell you this without hurting your feelings, so I'm just going to have to hurt your feelings. I don't
know where you classical guys get off thinking you can come
in here and play a kind of music that is completely outside,
above, and beyond your grasp. Just because your mom made
you practise some stuff for ten years does not mean that you
can waltz into an institution like *this* and play jazz, Rich. Jazz,
I'm talking. Because you can't. I got thirteen-year-old kids
from the projects who've never had a lesson, can't read a note,
they could wipe your white middle-class ass right off the keyboard. You want some good advice? Run, don't walk, back to
classical music. That's where you belong. I've read your re-
cords. You've done really well in the thingy—the festival—and
got high marks on your exams and that's great, but it means
diddly-squat here. Diddly. You really want to play pop music, do what everyone else does; go out, buy one of those big
fat books, *The Hundred Greatest Tunes of the Millennium* or
whatever, and when your friends are drunk at a party you
can play them something from *Cats*. That's about it for a guy
like you. I know this is brutal, but I want you to understand,
Rich, I'm actually doing you a favour here, okay? And I am
sorry, son. *(beat)* You wanna tell the next kid it's okay to come
in on your way out, I'd appreciate it.

            *TED walks away. RICHARD stands, lost in dismay, and
            finally exits.*

WHAT NOW? / MARSHA

We hear a ticking clock. TED *sits and plays/sings…*

TED   *She's late for her lesson. Maybe she's dead. I hope so.*

RICHARD   Oh Teddy! (*RICHARD enters.*) Oh, Teddy, I am so sorry. I am so late.

TED   That's all right.

RICHARD   The lesson's almost over, isn't it?

TED   Oh there's still time left, but we've got to stop right on time though, Mrs. Billingsley, there's someone coming right after you. They run a tight ship here at ABC.

RICHARD   Oh Teddy, I've had such a dreadful day.

TED   Oh boy.

RICHARD   I had to drive the children all over hell's half acre and I am feeling a little emotionally raw today.

TED   I'm very sorry about that, Mrs. Billingsley.

RICHARD   Oh please, Teddy, call me Marsha.

TED   What are we looking at this week?

RICHARD   (*pointing to his music book*) "In My Little Birch Canoe."

TED   Did you finish "Finger Fun"?

RICHARD   Yes, you see, you actually gave me a gold star last week.

TED   I think you put that there.

RICHARD   Oh Teddy. *(She starts to play.)*

TED   Whoa. Everybody out of the canoe. Mrs. B, what do I say every week? You have got to start remembering or I'm going to—I'm going to…

RICHARD   What, Teddy?

TED   I'm going to lose the will to live.

RICHARD   Oh Teddy, you're only seventeen.

TED   I do but jest. But seriously, there are three things that I say every week.

RICHARD   *(suddenly remembering)* Curve my fingers!

TED   That's one.

RICHARD   And lower my wrists! At the same time!

TED   That's two.

RICHARD   And count out loud while I play!! Oh, silly Marsha! *(RICHARD begins to play.)* One bit, two bit, three bit. *(RICHARD stops playing.)* Oh Teddy, Teddy, do you remember when I was telling you about my friend Peggy? Yes, you remember! She's the one who's been my best friend ever since high school when we were on the cheerleading squad together. Well, Peggy has been very depressed lately; I think she's going through the change…

           Lights down. TED *changes position. The clock ticks. Lights up.*

…And so I said to the clerk in that store, "There is no way I am going to pay $69.99 for that blouse!" It was kind of like the one I wore about three weeks ago, Teddy, do you remember, it had a floral pattern…

> *Lights down.* TED *changes position. The clock ticks. Lights up.*

…And then, when I was seventeen, just about your age, Teddy, I used to spend hours looking at my father's fossil collection. I always thought that one day I would be a paleontologist. Isn't it funny the way life turns out?

> *Lights down.* TED *changes position. The clock ticks. Lights up.*

My husband's having an affair. *(She cries uncontrollably.)*

TED   *(long beat)* That's about all the time we have, Mrs. Billingsley. I'm sorry, there's someone coming right after you.

RICHARD   I understand.

TED   I'm sorry about your troubles.

RICHARD   Thank you, Teddy.

TED   Um, we'll see you next week, okay?

RICHARD   I look forward to it. *(RICHARD exits.)*

TED   That was pretty good there for a sec.

> TED *sits at the stage left piano.* RICHARD *re-enters stage right, sits, and plays.* TED *exits.*

PIANO BAR

> RICHARD *sings a suitable song for a piano bar.* TED *enters talking on a cellphone with drink and cigarette in hand.* RICHARD *continues to play.*

TED   You sell when I tell you to sell, you buy when I tell you to buy—this is not a dialogue, asshole! *(He hangs up.)* I'll have another one of these, dollface, and I mean that politically correctly. Tell starboy to make it a double, will you? Hey, Paul, Paul, Paul, Paul, Paul, Paul, Paul, PAUL! Oh, sorry, I thought you were Paul. *(RICHARD finishes the song.)* Hey, that was great.

RICHARD   Thanks.

TED   How old are you there, little guy?

RICHARD   Seve... uh... nineteen.

TED   Yeah right, can I see some ID? *(RICHARD balks.)* Don't worry, I won't blow your cover. That was pretty good there, eh? I know music.

> TED *plays the knuckle-roll song on the piano.* RICHARD *takes his hand away.*

RICHARD   Thanks. So, do you have any requests?

TED   Do you know *(the name of the song he just played)*?

RICHARD   *(slumping with disbelief)* I just played it.

TED   What, in your last set you mean?

RICHARD   No. I *just* played it.

At the Tarragon Theatre, 1996.
Photo by Beatrice Campbell.

TED   No you didn't.

RICHARD   Yes I did.

TED   No you didn't.

RICHARD   Yes I did.

TED   I was standing right here.

RICHARD   Well, I played it right here.

TED   Are you calling me a liar?

RICHARD   No, I'm not calling you a liar—

RICHARD	I'll tell you though—maybe if you weren't yelling across the bar to Paul or talking on your cellphone, you might have heard—	TED	You think I don't know *(name of song)*? You'll tell me though?! I was listening to that song before you were born, you little underage smartass.

TED   You don't want to play the goddamn song, that's fine with me! Just say, "I'm sorry, sir, but I'd rather not play that particular selection at this juncture." And we move on!

RICHARD   *(trying to get him to quiet down)* Okay, okay. I'll play it again.

TED   You'll play it for the first time. *(RICHARD begins to play.)* Hey! *(RICHARD stops playing and looks at him.)* Say it.

> *RICHARD laughs. TED crosses over to him menacingly.*

You better say it.

RICHARD   I'll play it for the first time.

TED   Goddamn right! *(RICHARD begins to play.)* Yeah, that's *(name of song)*! *(beat)* I gotta to take a whiz, kid. *(TED exits.)* Gary! Gary! Sorry, I thought you were Gary…

> *RICHARD continues to play (name of song) until Mr. Scarlatti enters.*

MOVING ON

TED   Ricky, Ricky, what you do, eh?

RICHARD   Oh sorry, Mr. Scarlatti, I was just fooling around.

TED   That's-a *(name of writer of the previous song).*

RICHARD   Mr. Scarlatti. You know *(name of writer)*?

TED   Yeah. I like-a *(name of writer).* He's a man. He's a real man. He's a piano man.

RICHARD   That's a good one, Mr. S.

TED   Thank you.

RICHARD   So, how's your back?

TED   Not so good, how's your Bach?

RICHARD   Not so good.

TED   *(as he lies down)* What else have you got for me this week, Ricky?

RICHARD   Well, believe it or not, I'm still working on the second Chopin Ballade.

TED   Oh, she's a pig.

RICHARD   Yeah. Oh, I've got the Schoenberg.

TED   Oh no, no, no Shoenberg, I'm in the mood for a melody.

RICHARD   How about the Mozart Fantasia in C Minor?

TED   Give me the Bach. You play that for my back. My back likes that one. Take it from the cadenza, Ricky. The B flat. *(beat)* It's-a good for my back to "be" flat.

RICHARD   I don't know where you come up with them, Mr. S.

TED   It's a gift. *(RICHARD begins to play in a rush.)* Hey, hey, hey. Think before you play, Rambo. Breathe. Start again. *(RICHARD plays a segment, then stops.)* Ricardo. You play this better three weeks ago. What's-a matter? Think before you play. Breathe. Let's go. Start again. *(RICHARD plays one note then stops.)*

RICHARD   Mr. Scarlatti, I can't go on. I'm seventeen years old. I can't go on being a piano nerd. Sitting for hours on end in a room by myself trying to make my fingers do unnatural contortions. The piano's become like this millstone around my neck. I feel guilty when I'm not practising, I feel inadequate when I do. I'm not going anywhere as a classical pianist. You know it, and I know it. And anyway, how is it relevant? I want to work to change the world, Mr. Scarlatti. Politically. How am I going to do that being a classical pianist? Classical music is this middle-class, European, elitist art form that is dying in front of an apathetic public that gets more satisfaction playing Nintendo. And acoustic instrumentation is dead. I mean, no offence, Mr. Scarlatti, but the piano is going the way of the typewriter… or the eight-track cassette. And classical musicians are becoming this smaller and smaller cabal of crazy archaic artisans, like stonemasons or blacksmiths or something. I mean, we're weird now, but we're going to get weirder and weirder as we get fewer and fewer, until finally we'll be totally outside of society altogether. Cultural lepers. *(beat)* I just want you to know that this has nothing to do with you. I think you're a great teacher and a great guy. I've learned a lot from you… and not just about the piano. But it's time for me to move on. Mr. Scarlatti… *(long beat)* I'm quitting the piano.

Pause. A deep snore comes from Mr. Scarlatti. RICHARD *leans over him.*

We hear the finale of Horowitz's Carnegie Hall performance of the Mephisto Waltz by Liszt.

RICHARD   Ted. Ted!

TED   What?

RICHARD   Do you want another beer?

TED   Yeah, yeah. Shh. This is the part.

RICHARD   What part?

TED   The part I've been telling you about! It sounds like a Ping-Pong ball being dropped. *(RICHARD exits to get them a beer.)* How does he do that?! Here it comes again. Ping-Pong ball.

RICHARD *hands a beer to* TED; TED *crosses to his piano.*

Here he goes. Listen to this.

We listen to the end of the recording as TED *plays air piano along with Horowitz. At the end he cheers along with the crowd and collapses on the piano, listening to the applause as it fades.*

That, my friend, is one little seventy-five-year-old man, one big black piano, and two thousand people who would rather be there than anywhere else; whose lives were forever altered on that day, who still say today, "I was there when Vlad played Carnegie Hall." If you're not going to play like that what's the point? I think that's why I quit. I knew what I'd have to go through to play like that. What seventeen-year-old kid wants to sit in a little room by himself staring at little black dots, developing hemorrhoids? I was a social kid. I wanted to be out in the world with people, real live people. Interacting, you know? Now that people are such a big part of my life, I often wish I was in a little room by myself. Stupid thing is, now I know how to work. Now I've got discipline. Now I enjoy practising. Now it's too late. But some little part of me still thinks I could have done it. I could have been a world-class classical musician. I could have played Carnegie Hall. It's very important for me to believe that, because if I didn't believe that, it would mean that I didn't quit because I wanted a normal life, it'd mean I quit because I wasn't good enough. *(pause)* Shit, now I'm depressed.

RICHARD   Do you remember the last time we got this drunk together?

TED   Vaguely.

RICHARD   Well you put on that same CD of Vladimir Horowitz playing the Mephisto Waltz by Franz Liszt…

At the Tarragon Theatre, 1996.
Photo by Lydia Pawelka.

TED	Guilty, my lord.
RICHARD	…and you made the same fehschtunkineh speech you just did.
TED	I did not.
RICHARD	You did too.
TED	I did not.
RICHARD	You did too.
TED	*(beat)* Did I really?
RICHARD	Yep.
TED	That's pathetic.
RICHARD	Yep.
TED	Thanks, now I'm even more depressed. You know what I'm talking about though, don't you, Rich?
RICHARD	Yeah. *(beat)* But you know—we're not bad piano players.
TED	No, we're not *bad*.
RICHARD	We're okay.
TED	We're pretty good.
RICHARD	We're quite good.
TED	We're two of the best piano players in the world.
RICHARD	No, we're not.

TED   We're two of the best piano players in the country?

RICHARD   No, we're not.

TED   We're two of the best piano players in the city?

BOTH   *(beat)* No.

TED   In the neighbourhood?

RICHARD   Yes.

BOTH   We are two of the best piano players in the neighbourhood.

> *They contemplate this. They look at their hands. They look at each other. They get up and they put on their tuxedo tails. They check with each other that they're ready and sit down at their pianos together.*
>
> *They then play the first movement of the Bach D Minor Concerto as well as two of the best piano players in the neighbourhood can play it.*
>
> *The end.*

Ted and Richard in front of Persephone Theatre, Saskatoon,
during their first Canadian tour, 1997.
Photo by Beatrice Campbell.

Stage Manager extraordinaire, Beatrice Campbell, in front
of the Royal Alexandra Theatre, Toronto, 1998.
Photo by Ted Dykstra & Richard Greenblatt.

ACKNOWLEDGEMENTS

Beatrice Campbell; Celia Chassels; Jean and Chalmers Doane; Melanie Doane; Theo and Rosie Dykstra; Theo and Truus Dykstra; Mallory Gilbert; Luke, Natasha, William, and Amelia Greenblatt; Tanya Greve; Fiona Jones; Steve Lucas; Kate Lushington; Gloria Muzio; Robin McKim; the Ontario Arts Council; the Tarragon staff; and all of the people who attended and gave feedback on the first workshop of *2P4H*.

David and Ed Mirvish and all of those at Mirvish Productions who have supported the show throughout the years, Judy Richardson, Ben Sprecher and William P. Miller, and Rob Barg and the teams at Yamaha Canada and Yamaha Artist Services International.

A special thank you to Urjo Kareda for his dramaturgical input and support of the original production.

The playwrights would especially like to acknowledge Andy McKim's role as the consulting director of the original production. His input was, and is still, greatly appreciated.

Ted's professional career began in Edmonton at the age of fifteen. Since then he has gone on to play leading roles on every major stage in Canada, often combining his musical skills in such roles as Mozart in *Amadeus*; Cale Blackwell, a character based on Jerry Lee Lewis, in *Fire*; Shostakovich in *Master Class*; Glenn Gould in *An Evening with Glenn Gould*; Hedwig in *Hedwig and the Angry Inch*; and Cousin Kevin in *The Who's Tommy*. School children around the world know him as Bach in the film *Bach's Fight for Freedom*. He is also a veteran of both the Shaw and Stratford Shakespeare festivals. He has appeared in dozens of films and TV shows and has also voiced dozens of cartoon characters. In 2000 he turned his attention to directing, and has since helmed many award-winning shows across the country, notably for Soulpepper Theatre, of which he is a founding member. He has also directed *2 Pianos 4 Hands* across America and in Australia and Hong Kong. Recently, his performance and adaptation of Tolstoy's *Kreutzer Sonata* received accolades from critics and colleagues alike. He has received four Dora Mavor Moore Awards, a Gemini, an Elizabeth Sterling Haynes Award, a Robert Merritt Award, and a Chalmers Award for acting, writing, and directing.

All of the above, however, pales compared to being the proud father of Theo and Rosie.

Richard Greenblatt is an actor, director, writer, and musician who has been a professional theatre artist for almost four decades. He was born in Montreal and studied piano for ten years with the late Professor Dorothy Morton of the McGill Conservatory of Music. He received his acting training at the Royal Academy of Dramatic Art in London, England. Since returning to Canada, he has performed in theatres across Canada and abroad, as well as in feature films, television, and radio. He has directed well over one hundred productions for theatres across the country, the vast majority being original and/or Canadian works. He has also directed many classical works, as well as the premieres of groundbreaking and award-winning plays for young audiences.

As a writer, he wrote or co-wrote *2 Pianos 4 Hands*, *Sibs*, *The Theory of Relatives*, *i.d.*, *Letters from Lehrer*, *Care*, and *Soft Pedalling*. *2 Pianos 4 Hands* has played on five continents and in over two hundred cities since it opened at the Tarragon Theatre in April 1996. Greenblatt himself has performed the play with co-creator Ted Dykstra over 850 times across Canada and in New York City, Washington, DC, London, and Tokyo. He has taught acting, directing, and play creation at most of the theatre-training institutions in Canada.

He lives in Toronto with partner Tanya Greve and their daughter Amelia, and is the proud father of Natasha, Will, and the dearly missed Luke Greenblatt.

RECYCLED
Paper made from
recycled material
FSC® C103567

Printed on Silva Enviro 100% post-consumer EcoLogo certified paper,
processed chlorine free and manufactured using biogas energy.